SHARE
YOUR
BRILLIANCE

COMPILED BY
REBECCA HALL GRUYTER
#1 INTERNATIONAL BEST SELLING AUTHOR

Share Your Brilliance

Copyright © 2023 by Rebecca Hall Gruyter

RHG Media Productions
25495 Southwick Drive #103
Hayward, CA 94544

All rights reserved. No part of this publication may be reproduced distributed or transmitted in any form or by any means including photocopying recording or other electronic or mechanical means without proper written permission of author or publisher, except in the case of brief quotations embodied in critical reviews and certain other noncommercial uses permitted by copyright law.

ISBN 978-1-7374041-4-9 (paperback)

Visit us on line at www.YourPurposeDrivenPractice.com
Printed in the United States of America.

CONTENTS

Preface — By Rebecca Hall Gruyter, Compiler 5

Section 1: You Are Brilliant

I Am . . . — By Wendy L Hooton 11
Why Did This Happen For Me? — By Misti Mazurik 19
Be Bold. Explore Your Super Powers! — By Beverly Brunelle 27

Section 2: Claim Your Brilliance

You Are Not Alone! — By Beth McGill 41
Discover Your Creative Potential — By Bri Capirsi 49

Section 3: Share Your Brilliance

Leadership of Self: How We Show Up Is a Choice — By Dr. Cheryl Lentz 59
Share Your Gifts With the World: Interview Like a Pro — By Rebecca Hall Gruyter 69
Quotes to Encourage and Inspire You 81

Closing Thoughts — By Rebecca Hall Gruyter, Compiler 99

PREFACE

Thank you for leaning into this powerful anthology! We are honored and excited to bring you this powerful book featuring seven experts who are committed to helping you *Share Your Brilliance.*

Our vision is to have our experts share insights, tips, and tools we have discovered to support and empower you on your journey. We know that life is not a solo journey, and by coming together, our goal is to help you step further and more powerfully into your gifts, talents, and abilities. Together, as we lift each other up, we are all able to grow, reach more people, and have a greater impact than we do trying to do everything on our own.

In each chapter, our authors will equip and empower you to step forward more fully. We believe this book is a living and interactive book that will speak wisdom, encouragement, and power into your life. We want to invite you to pause, take a deep breath, and be ready to receive these powerful chapters so they can ignite a fire in you, inspire courage in you, and focus you on stepping fully into bringing forward the gift of who you are and all that you are called to be. Enjoy the inspirational quotes woven in throughout the book to inspire, encourage and motivate you.

Here is how to get the most out of this powerful book. The book is divided into three sections; each one is designed to meet you exactly where you are and to support you in each step of your journey. **In the first section, You Are Brilliant,** we help you connect more fully with yourself, your truth, and your brilliance. **In the second section, Claim Your Brilliance,** our experts share how to step into your gifts and talents and choose to live in a positive and empowered way by helping you fully claim your brilliance. **In the third section, Share Your Brilliance,** our experts share with you how to move forward with your purpose and shine your gifts out into the world. At the end of each powerful chapter, you will find the author's biography and contact information. We encourage you to "friend" and follow those authors with whom you feel a powerful resonance and connection so that they can continue to pour into you and support you on your journey in life.

Now the next step is yours. Drink in the insights, tips, and wisdom that are within these pages to serve, support, and inspire you. Take the time to pause, read, and reflect. Listen to the powerful messages of hope that are waiting for you within the pages of this book. It's not an accident that you purchased this book and are opening it to read. We invite you to lean in and truly receive the messages and wisdom that will speak to your heart and soul that you will find in these transformational and dynamic pages. Enjoy this rich collection of wisdom, insight, and encouragement being provided by our amazing authors. We can't wait to see you stepping into and shining in your brilliant purpose!

Rebecca Hall Gruyter, Compiler
Founder/Owner of Your Purpose Driven Practice and CEO of RHG Media Productions.

ACKNOWLEDGMENTS

When writing an anthology, it takes many voices willing to join together to bring forth the book in a powerful and united way. It has been such an honor and privilege to work with this amazing group of experts and influencers. We want to thank these amazing leaders for trusting us to bring forth and share their powerful stories.

Thank you to our amazing teams, communities, families, and friends for leaning in, cheering us on, and saying yes to help us bring this book forward so powerfully. It takes many hearts and spirits coming together, bringing their gifts and talents to the mix to bring something like this book forward in multiple formats. We thank the full team, community, authors, and readers for leaning in to support us in bringing this powerful book to the world. You make the journey brilliant by being on it with us.

SECTION 1:

You Are Brilliant

I AM...
BY WENDY L HOOTON

"**Y**ou must be special." *Huh? Why do people keep telling me that?*

When I think of *special*, I think of gifted. I think of a person who has an unbelievable talent that they share with the world. For instance, a person who can bring life to the black and white keys on a keyboard, making unbelievable music, like Sir Elton John. Or Celine Dion, whose angelic voice can bring people to tears as beautiful sounds spew from her vocal cords. *Special*, to me, is knowing exactly how to ingeniously combine shapes, colors, tones and textures to create a priceless painting.

I possess none of these skills—in fact just the opposite. When my fingers touch a keyboard, it sounds more like someone dropped a piano from the roof of a skyscraper. When I sing, it sounds like a trash compactor smashing its contents. Forget the thought of me painting when I can screw up something as simple as trying to draw a stick figure. No, I am a far cry from special . . . that is, as I interpret it.

So, what makes me special? Well, according to those who have mentioned it, it's my baby. My thirty-two-year-old big baby boy has labeled me as such.

He made me a mom at the young age of twenty-three, although that's old by Utah's standards. When my son entered the world three weeks early, he had the cutest and softest blonde mohawk, a tiny but mighty squeal, the correct number of appendages . . . and an extra chromosome in each cell of his body. My son had not only surprised us by arriving early, but we were also surprised with his unexpected Down syndrome diagnosis. I had little knowledge of Down syndrome. What I did know is that I did not want this for me or my baby. Shock and fear consumed me. I grieved for the baby I had been expecting but did not receive. I did not know how to move forward. *I am barely qualified to be a mom; how am I going to be a mom to a baby with special needs?* A dark cloud loomed over me, it felt like a storm trying to decide if it should pour or pass. With each day and every precious moment with my beautiful baby boy, I realized just that: he was a baby, *my* baby.

"He's beautiful! You know, God only sends these babies to special people." I heard from more than one visitor after his birth. *Why would they say that?* Truthfully, I didn't want to be special. I wanted to be normal, whatever normal was. My tears attempted to dry up as days turned into months. With my forced positive attitude, slowly the clouds began to lift.

Still, the birth of my precious baby meant I had to discover a power I didn't know I possessed: the strength that lived deep within my soul. I would need this to move forward in our journey. My world, my baby's world, would require a mom strong enough to take on the fight. A mom who could chase away bullies, who would be an ally with his doctors and specialists, and who would be his advocate when he began going to school and participating in extracurricular activities. He would be completely dependent on me to help him reach his greatest potential.

But how? I kept my umbrella close by as this weather, these storms, could be very unpredictable.

Fast-forward thirty years. On a hot Friday night in early July, my father and I sat in the emergency room of a local hospital. He hadn't been feeling well, so I took him to his doctor, who sent us over to the hospital for further testing. There was just enough room for a bed, a chair, and a computer in the small space we were in. There were two external doors on both sides of the room, almost as if it had been a closet at one time. From both entrances, I could hear the voices of nurses and doctors as they assisted other patients. I wished they were louder to drown out Dad's rants.

He raised me and my two younger brothers. He served in the military and was very strict. I'm not sure if it was because I was his only daughter, or because he had a military background. He was opinionated and passionate about his political beliefs and raised his voice whenever anyone disagreed with him. While I love my country and have my own opinions, I went about expressing mine differently than he did. He mistook this as meaning I didn't care. This made our relationship tumultuous, at times causing us to go months without seeing each other. He could be so much work, but I loved him.

That night as we sat in the hospital room waiting impatiently for someone to come and take a look at him, we watched TV. Big mistake. The news was on. I had wished his mouth were as weak as the rest of him. He went on and on about the president, loudly, until I got so tired of it that I finally cut him off and blurted out, "Dad, I love my birthday!" He stopped and looked at me with the most confused look on his weathered face. I went on.

"Dad, I don't feel like you know me. I feel you spend more time ranting about your political beliefs than taking the time to get to know who your daughter really is."

He stared at me through his big brown eyes.

"Do you know I spend each year giving back on my birthday?" I went into detail telling him how we would spend my day, the day he and my mom had given me life. I had his attention, for a minute. He listened intently and then he stopped me.

"Sweetheart, you don't have to tell me all of this. I know you're a good person. In fact, you're special." There's that word again.

"What do you mean?" I asked, wanting to know why my dad would say something that felt so unlike him.

"Wendy, I knew you was special the minute they laid your baby, my grandson, in your arms. The loving way you looked at him and how protective you've been of him from the very beginning." I teared up because this is not how my assertive dad usually spoke. "I know you're a good person and I'm proud of you."

After many years I finally felt validated by my dad. I knew what he thought of me not only as a person but as a mom. The tension that had once filled that room disappeared, like the nurse who had admitted us.

Sadly, within a month I unexpectedly lost my dad. I will forever cherish the conversation I had with him in that cold closet of a room. But the strength he instilled in me still exists.

Whether it was my dad or guests who may have been trying to help a grieving mother, I have never felt special. In fact, hearing this has always made me feel uncomfortable. I have felt it implies parents who did not have children with special needs, or even their children, were not remarkable in their own way. I had no unique gifts to make me more qualified for this job than any other mom I knew. In fact, I have known many moms who are much more qualified than me.

Then one day it hit me, like a bug on a windshield. They were all wrong. I had given birth to a child that a higher being knew I needed in *my* life, a child who would become my teacher. Not a teacher of academics, but a teacher of humanity. I have been working on getting my degree for the last thirty-plus years. My courses have been compassion, patience, acceptance, patience, kindness, patience and unconditional love—oh, and have I said patience? (I call this out because this is an area where I always scored the lowest.) I have had to ask for a hall pass a time or two, and there have been a few times I've had to skip recess and stay after school, but I've had the best teacher! I'm not failing, but there are days I know I need to study harder. Overall, I just hope my grade point average is better than what I received in school. I'm hoping for at least a 3.0.

We all have a story, don't we? Mine is no different from most. On more than one occasion, I've been told by others that they wouldn't know what to do if they were in my position. Heck, I didn't know what I was going to do. But we are all faced with difficult circumstances at some point in our lives, and we have two choices: accept it and do our best to work through it, or sulk in our misery. I am in complete support of sulking to some extent, even throwing pity parties. Lord knows I've thrown several of my own. I even bought a new couch that would be comfortable for these events. However, at some point, you have to clean up the confetti and toss the piñata and party hats because all parties must end eventually.

While I may not think I'm special, I'll tell you what I do believe: I am a superhero. Yep, that's right, I'm a freaking superhero. I say this with confidence now, but I haven't always felt this way. In fact, just the opposite. My self-esteem has been so low at times it could win any limbo dance contest. Doubt, fear and resistance are constantly inviting themselves to tag along on my journey; these three are my kryptonite. As soon as I acknowledge them, I have them escorted out . . . immediately! But none of this comes easily for me. It has taken my life experiences to help me realize that attitude is the difference between overcoming or succumbing. I have done both when faced with my personal tests. Attitude is my superpower—that, and humor.

For all the women reading this, you are all superheroes in my book. Yes . . . you are, it's just a matter of acknowledging your power and giving it some grace. Too many of us doubt ourselves. That's what I'm here for—I'm here to give you that nudge if you need it.

Life helps to prepare us, to arm us with our powers to overcome our obstacles. For me, what I originally believed to be a strict father was actually my Stan Lee, my own superhero creator. (Stan Lee is known for creating comic book superheroes). From the time I was a young girl, my dad had been training me, preparing me for the challenging future that lay ahead of me. Thanks to my dad's discipline, I had become tough. Thanks to watching him raise three kids on his own, I understood making sacrifices and living on a strict budget, even though I didn't always like it. Dad had instilled in me a sense of independence and, at the same time, responsibility. I would have to make tough decisions; good thing I was tough. These things and more were all key ingredients that helped enhance and feed my girl power. I needed these powers not only when I became a mom, but when, three years later, I became a single mom. Not a life I would have chosen for myself, but it's not one I would trade, either. I have felt myself become stronger with every challenge I have had. It's like they feed my powers. Dear Universe, do not misunderstand this as a request for more.

Thanks to my dad, and my son's extra chromosome, I am not only aware, but also, when I'm feeling daring, I flaunt my strength. Do you know why? Because I have an even bigger power behind me now . . . faith. I close my eyes and grab hold of its hand, allowing it to guide me freely. I trust it.

Never forget that you possess superhuman abilities too. But it's up to you to nourish them and believe in them. Don't ever let anyone determine your fate.

That's YOUR job. Remember the cape on your back when you find yourself resisting becoming the woman you are. YOU ARE STRONG!

Every morning when I open the door to my closet and stare at my rack of clothes, I ask myself: *So who am I today? Wonder Wendy or Super Mom?* It's a good thing my cape is reversible because I am . . . Wonder Wendy AND Super Mom—today and every day! So, I ask you, who are you today? Do you believe in yourself enough to acknowledge your power? I hope so . . . because I know you possess amazing strengths. Know that I am here cheering for you, and if you ever need encouragement, just reach out and I'll be happy to help you claim your superpowers and SHINE!

INSPIRATIONAL QUOTES PROVIDED BY WENDY HOOTON

"You never know how strong you are, until being strong is your only choice."
—Bob Marley

"Making a big life change is scary, but know what's even scarier? Regret."
—Zig Ziglar

"You weren't rejected. I hid your value from them because they were not assigned to your destiny.'"
—Unknown

"I've learned that people will forget what you said, people will forget what you did, but people will never forget how you made them feel."
—Maya Angelou

"Kindness is a gift everyone can afford to give."
—Unknown

At the end of each day Wendy Hooton asks herself: "What made me smile today? What are three things I'm grateful for? Did I live today, love today, matter today?"

Wendy L Hooton

Wendy is an author, speaker, Down syndrome advocate, and coach.

Wendy found her strength and her voice when she became a mom to her son, who at birth, surprised her with his Down syndrome diagnosis. She has thirty-two years of lived expertise and is passionate about sharing her incredible but unplanned journey. She is dedicated to helping new parents move beyond the shock and grief they might experience after learning of a newborn's unexpected prognosis. She aspires to help other women find their own strength and voice to speak up for themselves and their children.

Wendy has eighteen years of experience working with a nonprofit organization, where she learned leadership skills and developed ties with the community while offering support to families.

Prior to becoming an author, she spent thirty-five years with a Fortune 500 company. There she trained and mentored new team members and managed premier accounts while delivering outstanding customer service to CPOs and People Operations.

The day Wendy became a mom, she also became a teacher, a student and a warrior. She's fun, motivated, dedicated and fearless, which may be what qualified her for the position. When she is not lost in her writing or soaking up words written by other authors, Wendy enjoys spending time with her family and friends on adventurous road trips, at a beach, or driving through the majestic Utah mountains. Her favorite activity, though, is being entertained by her hilarious son.

Email: **whooton@comcast.net**
Website: **www.wendylhooton.com**
Facebook: **facebook.com/wendy.lhooton**
LinkedIn: **https://www.linkedin.com/in/wendy-hooton-1bb072148/**
Instagram: **https://www.instagram.com/peaceowendy/**

WHY DID THIS HAPPEN FOR ME?
BY MISTI MAZURIK

"Keep your face always toward the sunshine—and shadows will fall behind you."
—Walt Whitman

When we wake up in the morning, we have a choice: a choice to face the day with a positive attitude or a negative attitude. My choice each and every day is to be positive. Being positive is a choice, and it is also hard work. At least it is for me.

Every day we are bombarded with messages of positivity. It seems so simple, right? But is it really? Where is the plan to that positive state of mind?

I have a plan for a positive state of mind, and it works for me. But it takes work and self-analysis!

I want to live a positive life because life is so much better and you shine so much brighter when your glass is half full and NOT half empty. Like an amazing marriage or relationship, a positive attitude takes work. Everything in life worth having takes work and maintenance.

I remove sadness from my life. While I work at positivity and happiness, I do have an overall positive attitude. Sometimes we don't even recognize the sadness. I am an early riser, and it used to be that I would get up, get my husband off to work and watch an episode of my favorite show . . . *Grey's Anatomy*. While I love the show, I came to realize it was making me sad each and every day I watched it. All day I would think, *Why am I so sad?* Nothing was wrong, nothing had happened to make me sad, but yet I felt a residual sadness all day. And one day it hit me like a ton of bricks . . . *It's* Grey's Anatomy. *It's making you sad.* The sadness of the situations in this television show affected my outlook on my day and hence made me have less than a positive attitude. While I still consider *Grey's Anatomy* to be one of my favorite shows, I never watch it. And my positivity has skyrocketed, with no more residual sadness throughout my day. Pay attention to what you are watching and having in your environment. How is it helping you stay positive? How is it lifting you up? Or is it?

My name is Misti, and I overanalyze most things. I have been doing so for most of my life. Overanalyzing has a negative connotation to it, but it has led me to what I believe is my greatest discovery in life. In my opinion, I productively overanalyze. Which leads us to focus of this chapter . . . when something negative happens, I ask myself, "Why did this happen FOR me?"—not TO me. Sometimes the answer is not readily seen. You can go with the old standard, "What doesn't kill us makes us stronger." But initially so many things seem negative, but when viewed in hindsight they are actually a gateway to something amazing or at the very least informative.

The simple understanding that not everything happens to you but *for* you is very empowering. There is nothing more defeating than feeling like the victim, as if something is happening to you and you have zero control over it. Yet with a simple switch, you ask the question . . . Why is this happening For me? You switch from being a victim to instead receiving a potential gift. Even difficult moments have a gift in them if you look deeply enough and wait long enough.

How I met my husband is a great example of this principle. I had just attended my grandmother's funeral. Needless to say, I was heartbroken as she was also my very best friend in the world. I had months in advance committed to helping at a trade show as a favor for a friend. As you can imagine, my heart wasn't truly into this project; it was still raw and hurting from the passing of my grandmother. But I had committed to doing the show, so I was going to honor my commitment. I arrived at the trade show to set up the display and was immediately informed that my spot had not been paid for in advance. The trade show manager proceeded to tell me that he would not allow my company to be in the trade show if he wasn't paid by the next day. In that moment, I thought to myself: *I can tell this guy I don't intend to pay him and he would kick me out of the trade show and I could go home and mourn in peace. Or I can honor my commitment.* I chose to honor my commitment. In those moments I asked myself, "Why is this happening FOR me?" As I said before, the answer is not always readily seen.

What came from that honoring of my commitment and asking my simple question is more wonderful than I can ever put into words. Sometimes the little things lead to the biggest changes. After the initial interaction setting up the trade show booth, I settled in to my show space, right across from the trade show manager's booth. This was it. My 20' × 20' plot to spend the next ten days of my life. I was not looking forward to the ten days ahead of me, but I had made a commitment. It was loud, harshly lit and not very comfortable by any measure. I had two folding chairs to rotate with my coworkers. There was also the floor. Oh, the floor. A giant slab of concrete as far as the eye could see. Being a professional meant dressing for the job. Professional attire meant professional shoes . . . a.k.a. heels. Not very comfortable on that hard floor.

I was to find out later that these heels changed my life. Any time I walked around, my heels made a distinct clicking noise on the hard concrete. This did not go unnoticed. At first the trade show manager was distracted by the clicking. I later found out this evolved into a calling. Every time he heard the clicking, his attention was directed in my direction. That clicking was my siren. After watching from afar for couple of days, he was overwhelmingly compelled (his words) to ask me on a date. We will be married ten years in just a few short months. It took a concrete floor, heels, and a trade show forty miles from home to change my life forever. That trade show manager, who was upset with me and threatened to kick me out of the trade show, became my husband. Had I sat and felt sorry and played the victim and not honored my commitment, I would have missed out on finding the love of my life. So, while it was an awful situation, there was a silver lining and it happened FOR me, not TO me.

My plan to live a positive life is nothing more than examining the things that happen. **This simple question: "Why did this happen FOR me?" can be applied to the mundane as well as the monumental things that happen in life.** I always keep in mind that it is not happening to me. It's empowering, and it makes a difference. Not all that looks bad on the surface is bad. Sometimes things that happen are blessings in disguise, and it is up to us to find that blessing.

Here is another example: Many years ago, I was involved in a relationship for many years with someone who did not treat me the way that I deserved to be treated. I was a prisoner in a relationship that I wanted to just go away. I tried everything to leave the relationship, but to no avail. He would not have it. If he wasn't ready for the relationship to end, then it would not end. This went on for several years, and I endured his accusations, his breaking into my house, the many tires he slashed, stealing my identity, and the thousands of other little things he did to make my life miserable. Finally, my future husband ended this situation by simply being a presence in my life. For this I am forever grateful. Why did this happen FOR me? It happened FOR me so I could see and know what an amazing relationship feels and looks like. Would I have had the same appreciation for my husband if I had not seen what a truly ugly relationship looks and feels like? It is why that situation happened FOR me, not TO me.

A few years ago, I volunteered as the marketing director for my local Relay for Life. I remember working on a fundraiser that we hoped would be an amazing success. Sadly, we could not sell the tickets that were required to fill the event, and we had to cancel it. I was devastated that this event had been cancelled. So much time and energy wasted. Or was it? Why did this happen FOR me? Again, I began analyzing. Why were we not able to fill such an amazing event for such a worthy cause? The answer became crystal clear! The conclusion I reached was that we were not reaching the entire area that our Relay for Life encompassed. We were not targeting our entire market, and some felt that it wasn't an event for them. Instead of feeling defeated, I set out to create a marketing campaign that made each and every area that we covered feel a part of the mission. And from this also came national recognition from the American Cancer society for our marketing campaign. Why did it happen FOR me? So that we could improve something and make it even better to include more people!

The concept of asking "Why did this happen FOR me, not TO me" is being proactive, and it IS empowering. Many situations feel negative at first glance. If we are courageous enough to look deeper, we can gain knowledge about ourselves when we encounter things that are difficult. Change and overcoming obstacles are never easy things, but they are necessary parts of life. Asking the simple question that I propose puts you in charge of the change!

Recently, I have accepted that I am an empath. I do not believe that this is something that is a supernatural power; rather, I believe it is being aware and in tune with others around you—and, yes, having empathy. I feel this is why I need to work just a bit harder to maintain my positivity. Asking my question has saved my sanity. Conversely, I have come to accept that there are certain things in this world that I am not meant to understand.

Do you ever hear something that just makes you shake your head and wonder if you heard something correctly? People treating people horribly? The awful things that people say so cavalierly, never giving a second thought to having hurt or offended someone? I always tried to figure those people out. I wanted to understand their thought process. It made me sad that they were like they were, and I wanted to understand so badly. Then one day I realized I cannot change them, AND . . . here's the big AND . . . If I understood their thought process, I would have the same mindset as they do. Why do I bring this up? Being an empath can be emotionally draining. I choose to not take on negative ways of being. Instead, I choose to be mindful of how I show up. If they can ripple out negative energy, how can I ripple out positive? Why did this happen FOR me?

I believe that if I can make the tiniest difference in someone's life, then anything I must go through is worth it. Sometimes all it takes is a smile to make a difference in a stranger's day. Sometimes it is lending an ear. Being an empath at first glance is a negative. But I don't see it that way. I see it as a gift each and every day! And my simple question has given me new perspective and a way to deal with the emotions that I feel each and every day!

When you wake up tomorrow, what will you choose: positivity or negativity?

Why did this happen FOR you?

INSPIRATIONAL QUOTES PROVIDED BY MISTI MAZURIK

"Life is not measured by the number of breaths we take, but by the moments that take our breath away."
—Maya Angelou

"There are three ways to ultimate success: The first way is to be kind. The second way is to be kind. The third way is to be kind."
—Mister Rogers

"Perfection is not attainable. But if we chase perfection we can catch excellence."
—Vince Lombardi

"The way I see it, if you want the rainbow, you gotta put up with the rain."
—Dolly Parton

"The two most important days in your life are the day you are born and the day you figure out why."
—Mark Twain

"Nothing is impossible. Even the word itself says, 'I'm possible!'"
—Audrey Hepburn

"Broken just means that there are more pieces to share."
—Misti Mazurik

Misti Mazurik

Misti Mazurik holds a master's in political science from California University of Pennsylvania and is a certified teacher. She considers herself to be a Jill of all trades, as she has worked in many different fields from sales and marketing to human resources. But her joy is working with authors and her amazing coworkers at RHG Media Productions as the director of operations.

She believes to live a positive life is to live a happy and fulfilled life. She incorporates her "Why did this happen *for* me?" principle in her everyday life and lives blissfully every day!

What sparks the most joy for her is her family. Her family includes her husband of ten years, her four cats and her RHG Media Productions family, as well as the gaming community that she belongs to.

Misti can be reached on LinkedIn at https://www.linkedin.com/in/misti-mazurik/

BE BOLD. EXPLORE YOUR SUPER POWERS!
BY BEVERLY BRUNELLE

I am an Intuitive, quantum energy healer, teacher and author. I have been passionately exploring spirituality, energy healing and intuition development since 1986. The deepening journey started when I was invited to a weekend metaphysical conference with a friend. She and I had been reading with great curiosity: *The Road Less Traveled*; *Good-Bye to Guilt*; Louise Hay and Shirley MacLaine. I found my mind was opening to new realities and possibilities I had never considered.

One day my friend sent me a *Far Side* card with a drawing of a herd of sheep grazing in a meadow. One sheep was standing up on its back legs, reaching to the sky, bellowing: "We don't need to just be sheep!" That said it all. We had been living in a communal trance. Now, we were on a strong self-discovery journey that raised new questions, and we had no idea where it all was going to take us.

My friend was excited for us to go to a metaphysical conference nearby, because well-revered authors and experts from the States and the UK were presenting.

I had never been away from my two young children before, and I didn't want to go away for the weekend. She persisted. It became a very challenging choice. I ended up joining her.

It proved to be an intensive experience beyond expectation and explanation. The first day we dove deep into meditation. It was a bit concerning because I had vivid visions of demons, Christ, and drunken Irishmen flying through the room. The visions came into the night, even when I was not in meditation. I felt, and was, out of control. The next day I decided to participate in a class to learn how to help spirits in the astral planes move into higher frequencies. I thought this would help me.

There were about fifty of us in a large circle. The teacher set the stage by telling us that when people die suddenly, they are in shock and may not know they are actually dead. Others may have unfinished emotional issues that keep them earthbound. She guided us into a meditation and called those in spirit, in need of help, to speak through one of us. Silence prevailed.

Then suddenly, the energy came through ME! I was terrified because the man had died by electrocution. I felt everything. I didn't know what was him and what was me. I sat there in a full-blown experience of mega-flows of electricity moving through my body. The instructor came over. I was crying hysterically. It took a while, but she told me I was safe and didn't need to experience his suffering in order to do this spirit rescue. She guided me to disengage from his electrifying experience and bring him into a higher resonance of self-awareness, love and new freedom. It was extremely challenging.

I had never ever experienced such a wild ride. The whole event resolved and dissolved, and he was brought into the higher realms. I was in awe and felt spent.

The next day I returned to her class. She gave us the same guidance. And surprise: the spotlight was again on me. This time I became a very sad elderly woman. The woman revealed she had not said good-bye to her grandson before she died and wanted to tell him she loved him.

"What's your grandson's name?" the instructor asked.

"James."

"Is anyone here named James?"

A man across the room raised his hand. (I get chills right now as I remember and write this.)

The instructor invited James to come over to his "grandmother." She guided a heartfelt conversation between them. They both cried. We all cried. When they felt complete, the instructor guided the women to go to the highest light. There was a great calm in the room and in me. We all hugged. It had been such an intimate and mind-blowing experience.

Question your assumptions. Honor your true yes and no.

Weeks after that conference, drunken Irishmen were still coming to me daily, in my kitchen. I would move them to the highest light, but I felt out of control and afraid. I couldn't tell anyone. It was too weird. I decided to take classes with the woman who presented at the conference. She told me I needed clearer boundaries. I was stunned that it was okay to say "no" to these entities. And perhaps elsewhere in my life.

What I didn't realize was that I had no boundaries in my everyday life as well. I didn't trust my true inner yes and no. I also had a very sensitive awareness system. I wish I had noticed the correlation and had the capacities to honor myself more.

I began taking classes in meditation, channeling, intuitive medicine and exploring energy healing. Before we would start class, the teacher advised us students not to ask for a specific entity to channel, that those on the other side were very busy with many more important situations than visiting with us.

After many months I felt frustrated. It didn't make sense to me that beings on the other side were limited. It seemed to me they were multidimensional and could be in many places at the same time. I wanted to test out my hypothesis.

Be Curious. Ask Bold Questions and Experiment. What Are Your Super Powers?

This was the beginning of deepening my curiosity in metaphysics, bold experimentation, and extensive study, which continues to this day. Big questions arose: What is Possible? What am I capable of? I felt this was important for me to learn as well as for all of humanity: What are people capable of that is outside our everyday conditioning and expectations? What natural quantum powers, creative avenues and magic are available to each of us which we were not taught to explore? What magnificent creative quantum powers do we all have? And how can we wake them up with the intention to have a healthier world of self-love, honorable relationships and new life-changing possibilities? I believed if I could discover my super powers, anyone could. I felt compelled to explore.

The next conference took me into the world of past lives and a potent hypnotherapy session, which revealed more than my last three years of biweekly psychotherapy had barely touched upon. I was in awe at the immense new resource to reveal and heal. I was hooked. I became a hypnotherapist and past-life regressionist. I loved facilitating clients' self-discovery. I learned that healing the "past," i.e., the origins of our issues, dynamically heals the present. And, accessing the wisdom of a higher future expands our present perspectives and possibilities.

What Trances Are You In?

I am passionate to uncover what is unconsciously influencing, limiting and controlling us—what keeps us away from living our fuller Essence. What capacities do we have to bring love and honor to reveal, resolve and dissolve the origins of our repetitive patterns that cause us and others suffering? How can we be more honest with ourselves and each other, be more resourceful and create new capacities to thrive living in our higher vibrational states?

Through, meditation, quantum energy work, journaling, more questioning and curiously exploring my own limiting beliefs, expectations, assumptions and judgments, I have developed a lifestyle of teaming with the unknown, with the highest frequencies to infuse life with love and to wake up from the trances of living unconsciously.

This is what I help clients do so that they can discover the power within them to shine their truth, their creativity and their brilliance more fully within themselves, their relationships, their work and the world.

I have been amazed at how insidiously and powerfully our early development and ancestral traumas influence who we see ourselves to be, how we act, and how we perceive others and the world. We all have been conditioned into limiting trances that have been widely accepted as the norm.

Since those early explorations, I have trained in depth and worked with many masters in the fields of energy healing, meditation, intuition development, breath and sound healing, channeling, and more. For over thirty-five years my passionate curiosity for what is possible has taken me deeply into quantum physics, metaphysical studies, and travels into mystical India, Europe, Mexico and South America. I have helped thousands of people tune into their essence energy, love, clarity and wisdom within, often opening flows of heartfelt tears.

My experience is that all time is now. Our ancestry and early development from conception through young adult are informing us now: how we see ourselves, others and the world. It influences what we believe to be true and possible . . . until we question it and ourselves!

A client came to me concerned about resentment toward her close friend. We did a multidimensional life exploration and found the origins of the situation. We approached it with respect and love, and we energetically resolved the dispute, reaping great insights. Later, she reported they were on fabulous terms.

Your words are powerful. You can choose new words that raise your vibration and change your life. But first you have to listen, with an open mind, to what you are actually and perhaps automatically saying.

I have gone through long, challenging periods of deep depression. Some refer to such times as "the dark night of the soul." I found great support to open my mind to new possibilities from the writings of Florence Scovel Shinn. Her affirmations changed my life.

"Expect the unexpected. My seemingly impossible good now comes to pass. I am awake to my good. I am unmoved by circumstances, therefore circumstances move." I started to read them often, daily. I always felt better. They shifted my focus to a higher vibration. After years of this, I felt it was important to update her inspiration and express my own voice. For several weeks, I wrote downloads of information about how our power to choose dynamic words can create new possibilities and snap us out of the limiting trances we do not even know we are in. We are powerful beyond our dreams. When we truly listen to ourselves, we will hear our limiting expectations and how we are casting spells that keep us stuck, repeating and expecting the same disappointments. When we choose new words, new directions and new inspiration, we create potent change that truly supports us to flourish! The book is forthcoming!

My friend said she felt hopeless in her relationship. "He doesn't listen to or respect me." I encouraged her to choose words that draw out her core strength to claim her power: "I value and respect my inner authority." And she saw positive changes.

Be Honest With Yourself.

It is important to be clear with your intentions to create communication that matches what you truly want to invite into your experience. It is important to listen astutely to your speech to notice what is automatic, negative, complaining or blaming that is keeping you in a cycle of seeming limitation.

It is key to be honest with yourself and your desires. Claim it and then let it all go. This creates space for life to come to you in new ways. Holding on to expectations in fear infuses the essence of your intention and limits your awareness to perceive and receive new options and cues that life brings you.

Things Are Not As They Seem.

During the weeks before my mother died, I found myself automatically doing my version of Ho'Oponopono. There are four specific steps in the original version: I'm sorry, forgive me, thank you, I love you. For many nights I lay in bed in meditation, organically reviewing my life experiences with my mother. I apologized for my rudeness, resistance, anger and resentment. I apologized for butting in on my parents' arguments, thinking I knew how to fix things. I apologized for not understanding her. I didn't ask her to forgive me; I thanked her for giving me the opportunity to see more clearly where I was off, wrong, out of line, full of assumptions and know-betters. I humbly felt the pain, suffering and helplessness within me from those younger years. I began to see myself, and her, with fresh and compassionate eyes. I needed to forgive myself. I realized I had unconsciously been using my judgmental perceptions of her to hold me back, to keep me small and, ultimately, unconsciously and erroneously, to keep me safe.

I offered apologies to myself and to my mom for not having the capacities to communicate with greater self-awareness, compassion and respect. I thanked her for holding such a strong space for me to discover myself. I was in a state of love and gratitude with her and with my passionate younger self.

Several weeks after she died, I was cleaning out her bureaus, admiring how she cared for her things. Suddenly, I felt her presence as a powerful radiance that filled and surrounded me. I sat down, and my mom began communicating with me telepathically. "I hurt being the me, that you knew. I wanted you to feel my love and caring in ways that I truly felt. But I was more loyal to my predetermined limiting role that I agreed to before birth than I was to my Essence shining through in my relationships. I believed my loyalty was honorable even though I saw my role caused much pain. I didn't know I had a choice to change. Let that not be true for you or for anyone. You are truly not trapped in original loyalties. You are free to make new choices on how you want to be."

The transmission was so strong. It is still in me.

What Are You Mistakenly Loyal To?

I realized I had a lifetime of locking myself into narrowly self-defined roles of daughter, wife, mother, teacher, writer, healer, etc. I wondered: What have I been mistakenly loyal to? What new choices are here for me now? The limitations of my original loyalties, like my mom's, were always made with good intentions. The choices were once right, yet had become blinding.

This is what I help clients do: I open their awareness to what is limiting them and help them to access their own wisdom, creativity, freedom and inner power.

If I knew then what I know now, I would have told myself:

Discover and live your authentic you!

~Be curious.

~Ask bold questions.

~Be outrageously honest with yourself.

~Trust and honor your boundaries: your clear nos and clear yeses.

~Experiment. Let yourself shine!

INSPIRATIONAL QUOTES PROVIDED BY BEVERLY BRUNELLE

"I am unmoved by circumstances, therefore circumstances move."
—Florence Scovel Shinn

"I am awake to my good and my good is awake to me."
—Florence Scovel Shinn

"My good comes from expected and unexpected sources."
—Florence Scovel Shinn

"My good now flows to me in a steady, unbroken, ever-increasing stream of success, happiness and abundance."
—Florence Scovel Shinn

My source of inspiration is often self inquiry because the right question in the moment can open new possibilities.
If I were boldly honest with myself....

*What am I assuming? How do I truly feel?
In an ideal world what would I prefer, want, need?
What questions will invite new possibilities?
What higher vibrational magic am I capable of?*

QUOTES BY BEVERLY BRUNELLE

"Your thoughts and feelings have the power to deeply nurture you. Be aware and make choices that please and perhaps even surprise you."
—*Luminous Infusions,* Beverly Brunelle

"Call upon your future joy and success to guide you and act as a team."
—*Luminous Infusions,* Beverly Brunelle

"Let go to the experience of yourself unfolding. Make nothing wrong. Just open to it. Allow your self to be surprised."
—*Luminous Infusions,* Beverly Brunelle

Beverly Brunelle

For over thirty years, I have been working in the fields of energy healing and human potential. My ongoing passion is discovering, "What are we capable of affecting in the quantum fields?" to make our lives better.

I am a Pioneering Master Energy Healer, Intuitive, teacher, speaker, writer and author. My mission is to support humanity awakening to its true power, presence and purpose.

My work empowers clients to heal generational and early developmental trauma to align more deeply with their inner wisdom and creativity.

I support people to shift from living unconscious limiting beliefs, perspectives and expectations to dynamically awaken their authentic powers of curiosity, clarity and freedom. I am certified in over seventeen modalities of healing arts. I offer online classes in intuition development, channeling, meditation, energy self-care, sacred relationship, ancestral healing and more.

My quantum energy work wakes up the personal fire of mysticism and higher intelligence in clients' lives. I facilitate individuals, couples and groups to create a new energy resonance within themselves and their past to open to fresh new possibilities for their current life and their most vibrant future.

My book *Luminous Infusions: Wisdom to Inspire Self-Awareness, Discovery and Empowering Change* is a compilation of my nature photographs, self-reflective guidance, meditation and journaling prompts. Together they offer heartfelt, uplifting perspectives and grounding guidance to go deeper into self-inquiry.

I write a monthly column for **TheInnerVoiceMagazine.com**; present regular online classes, meditations and energy healings; and am available for podcasts, workshops and speaking engagements. I offer private sessions for individuals, families and business groups worldwide.

Email: **beverlybrunelle888@gmail.com**
Website: **www.beverlybrunelle.com**
Facebook:
Beverly Brunelle Quantum Resonance Energy Healing,
facebook.com/people/Beverly-Brunelle-Quantum-Resonance-Energy-Healing/100089566907924/

LinkedIn:
www.linkedin.com/in/beverly-brunelle-3aa8a9110
YouTube:
youtube.com/@beverlybrunelle3981
Soul Search directory:
www.soulsearch.io/beverly-brunelle/united-states

SECTION 2:

Claim Your Brilliance

YOU ARE NOT ALONE!
BY BETH MCGILL

My name is Beth McGill, and I am a hypnotherapist, energy worker, speaker, teacher, best-selling author, wife, mom, grandma, gardener, nature lover, hiker and surfer. I live at the beach with my husband of fifteen years. We have a home in the mountains (because we love the mountains) and a vacation home in Baja (because we love the desert a lot). I'm fit, toned and strong. I am sixty-two years young and do not have any doctors, nor do I take any medication. Instead, I meditate every morning and clear my chakras—doesn't everybody? I am doing work in the world that I love because I love helping others feel better. I live my life in joy and bliss, and I want to show others how they can, too. I'm fully showing up in my life with passion and purpose, knowing that I am listening to and following the calling of my soul.

However, this hasn't always been the case. After college, I had a few good jobs, but I wanted to be my own boss. I had an *entrepreneurial spirit*. By the time I was thirty, I had two failed businesses—my fitness center and my real estate brokerage firm—and a whole lot of 'real world' experience. Then, at thirty, I had my first son, Kory. When he was barely three weeks old, I called my alma mater and asked them if I could come back and get my teaching credential. I needed a *real job*. They said yes. In the next year and a half, I received both my teaching credential and my second son, Kyle. In a couple more years, I was teaching second grade and living on a ranch in the country with my kids. My boys' father left the country to 'get work' and never returned. So now I was a single mom, and I kept teaching to raise my sons, to bring in a paycheck. It really was a good career for twenty years.

I was helping others, but I always felt a deep desire to help more people. The question, "How can I help more people?" kept ringing in my head. While I was still teaching full-time, another wonderful opportunity came my way, and I became a financial advisor. It was fun to be able to provide financial education to my friends and family, teachers, and then other families. As it turns out, I was very good at helping folks understand about investments and saving money, and my business took off. Slow at first, but within five years I left teaching to full fill my dream of working from home and being my own boss. Finally! I worked really hard to get there, and I kept working on my business to make it successful. I was helping a lot more people now, but at what price? I thought that my business had to get bigger to be better, I had to build a team, and I had to get more clients. As I focused on building my business, I lost sight of me. I was sacrificing my joy for others' definition of success. When I became aware that I was doing this, however, I decided to do something about it.

One day, I had an idea and I set my timer on my phone for five minutes and was quiet. I asked God, "Who Am I?" I knew that I was more than a financial advisor, mom, sister and wife, and I wanted an answer. As I sat there listening and asking, a word literally popped into my head. Turns out I'm clairaudient; who knew? I kept up my 'silent practice' for about ninety days, and then I realized at some point that I was on a *spiritual journey*. I was discovering who I was, tapping into my intuition, listening to and following the calling of my soul. It felt amazing.

I've been on this journey for a few years now, and a lot has changed in my life. I am living a life I love in a joyous state of appreciation and gratitude. **The most important shift that I experienced was when I realized** *I am an infinite spiritual being having a temporary physical experience, not the other way around.* This shift came about after lots of reading, studying, listening and allowing myself to open my mind to new thoughts, ideas and beliefs about the world and my role in it. It came about after I questioned everything. **And since I'm a spiritual being having a physical experience, I learned how to connect with my spiritual side, my soul. Then, I understood that** *I am never alone in my life experience, and neither are you.*

One of my earliest childhood memories is when I was around five or six. Growing up in my dear Quaker church, one of the first things I learned in Sunday school was that we spend eternity in Heaven after we die. This idea of *forever* really bothered me. I don't think that I've ever shared this before, but I vividly remember sitting on my bathroom floor, curled up like a ball, with a sick feeling in my stomach that wouldn't go away. I didn't understand how we could live in Heaven *forever*. My young mind wanted to figure it out but couldn't. How long is forever, anyway? I felt isolated and afraid. How could the world be this big and scary and confusing? Knowing what I know now, if I could go back in time and whisper in her tiny ear, I would tell her, "You are not alone, and you'll figure it out. You are going to be just fine."

When I was nineteen years old, I was attending college and playing tennis on the tennis team. I was in pretty good shape, but the coach told me that I needed to lose weight to compete. She had no idea what was going on in my personal life (it was a lot), but she didn't care. I decided to show her. I not only lost a lot of weight, but I also eventually became anorexic. I left school and never played tennis again. A couple of months later my boyfriend asked me to meet him at a park. It was a lovely warm day. I had no idea that my world was going to crash in around me. He broke up with me because he couldn't handle my not eating, and, more importantly, my personality changes due to the disease. And just like that, the love of my life was gone. He was right in that I had changed a lot. Anorexia is like that. It takes over your life. The next few months were horrible. I couldn't work. I couldn't do anything, but I managed to stay alive. If I could go back in time and whisper in her ear, I would tell her, "You are not alone, and you'll figure it out. You are going to be okay."

Now, I don't know what you are going through. Perhaps you are experiencing your own calling of your soul, and this is good confirmation. Or perhaps you are in a dark place, and you need to hear, **"You are not alone!" Wherever you are . . . your soul is leading you, guiding you, inspiring you, listening to you, breathing life into you and so much more. Isn't it time for you to listen to your soul so that you can have more peace, power and purpose in your life?**

That's right, you can have more peace in your life. That's exactly what happens when you connect to who you really are. For me it started with my 'silent practice,' which transitioned into a meditation practice. Meditating is simply the quieting of your mind. I highly suggest that you try it. You may ask a question like I did—"Who Am I?"—or you may come up with your own question. There are many types of meditation. It looks different for all of us. Experiment and see what feels right for you, but at the beginning keep it simple and focus on connecting to your soul.

When you start to meditate and you connect to God, Spirit, Universe, Source, Infinite Intelligence (whatever term you use is good), you start to feel energy flowing through you. You'll feel your own connection to your soul and your connection to the Universe. When you sense this, you'll begin to shift from living with a fear-based mindset to a mindset of faith and knowing. You'll come to realize that everything is always working out for you. That was my first mantra/affirmation and one that I still say today and everyday—*Everything is always working out for me*! Life becomes magical when you realize that the Universe is always showing you things, demonstrating things to you, and creating a path for you to give you everything that you desire. **When you accomplish this state of knowing that everything is working out for you, then you discover true peace in your life.**

Allow yourself this time to listen, and you will also discover that the Universe has a sense of humor. It is playful and fun. I am constantly asking the Universe for signs that everything is working out for me. In fact, while I was preparing for this project, I was also being led to offer a challenge to go with my *Allow Life to Happen 129 Day Journal*, which I just published on Amazon. My message was to start the challenge on April 25th and run the full 129 days. When I counted out the days it took the challenge to August 31st, which is the day that this book is going to launch. What perfect timing! I couldn't have planned it that way, but the Universe delighted me again. Things like this are happening all the time, and it reminds me to have fearless faith in the Universe and in myself.

When you achieve this connection to your soul and are living in fearless faith, you are not only in a peaceful state, but you also begin to understand that you are a powerful being. This power is already inside of you, and as you connect to your soul, you begin to remember your inherent self-worth. You understand that you are already worthy of living a life you love, and you begin to stand in your power. One of the ways that your newly found power shows up in your life is in your ability to make decisions with confidence. You begin to make decisions quickly and change your mind slowly.

I'll admit that it took me a while to understand this power inside of me and to claim it, but I'm going to share with you how I did it. First, I meditated consistently: first for five minutes, then ten, then fifteen to twenty minutes daily. My deep desire was to have a personal relationship with my soul. Immediately after

I meditated, I journaled. One day, I decided to write about what I expected my day to look like. For example:

> I am happy and grateful for every day that I am given, and I will live today to help and serve others. I am given new opportunities each day. Today is going to be an amazing day.

> Today I am feeling wonderful. I am energetic, enthusiastic, and looking forward to this amazing day. I am attracting more and more abundance into my life. Today is going to be a great day!

I journaled like this for a year or so. When I started my business Thrive Flourish & Grow, I decided to compile these journal prompts into a gift, hoping that they would inspire others to journal too. You can get your free copy of my 100 Inspirational Writing Prompts on my website at **www.thriveflourishgrow.com**.

As I kept journaling these positive expectations, wonderful things started happening in my life. I began to understand that I AM A POWERFUL CREATOR, and this power resides inside of me. I create MY REALITY! No situations, conditions, economy, government or others can take away my innate power. It's mine! You too are a powerful creator. What reality are you choosing to create?

Are you accepting that you are a spiritual being having a physical experience? Do you believe that you can live in a peaceful state, knowing that you are a powerful creator? I know you can, because I've experienced it. And I have one more thing to share with you. There is another upside for connecting with your soul. When you connect with your soul, you will discover your soul's calling. Earlier in this chapter, I shared that I was a financial advisor when I started my spiritual journey. I wasn't looking for another career, but my soul had other ideas. I started to pay attention to what I really loved and what I really wanted. I loved learning about the law of attraction, abundance and prosperity. I quickly realized that I wanted to teach this material. Then I discovered my gift for energy healing. A year later, I became a certified hypnotherapist and created my own healing modality, called H.E.A.L. Because I had this close relationship with my soul, I was able to establish a peaceful existence, where I stood in my power, and I allowed in all that I am being called to do. And I continue to follow my soul's calling every day as I trust my intuition and I trust in myself. This is my journey. My journey is to serve others while living my life in joy and bliss.

What about your journey? Are you ready to connect to your soul and to your true power? Are you ready to go with the flow and discover your purpose in life? Remember, everything that you are seeking is already inside of you. You must be willing to look within. I suggest you meditate and write in a journal daily. I've done many other processes and exercises, but at the end of the day, those are my two non-negotiables. Won't you give it a try?

It's imperative that I share one more thing here. Once you establish the connection to your soul, you will understand that you don't need to be concerned with the *how* and the *why*. You don't need to figure anything out. You will know that everything is working out for YOU! In his book *Manifest Your Destiny*, Wayne Dyer writes, "The secret to being patient is in the certainty of the outcome." When you know that everything is working out for you, your life becomes one of ease and flow and infinite patience.

Remember, you are not alone! I am here to guide and to serve you through educational online courses and/or powerful individual H.E.A.L. sessions. You can learn more by going to **www.thriveflourishgrow.com**.

With love, light, and JOY!
Beth

INSPIRATIONAL QUOTES PROVIDED BY BETH MCGILL

"Let go of having to know HOW it's going to get done. The universe has it all figured out already. Don't be concerned about the outcome. Instead, allow life to happen for you and through you. Allow it all in—joy, abundance, success, prosperity, love and fun!"
—Beth McGill

"Manifesting and meditating cannot be separated. They are like the crest and the trough of the wave, separate and distinct from each other, but always together. You cannot become adept at manifesting the desires of your heart if you are unwilling to devote time to the practice of meditation."
—Wayne Dyer

"There is for each man, perfect self-expression. There is a place which he is to fill and no one else can fill, something which he is to do, which no one else can do; it is his destiny!"
—Florence Scovel Shinn

"People do not attract that which they want, but that which they are."
—James Allen

"Nothing in life is to be feared, it is only to be understood. Now is the time to understand more, so that we may fear less."
—Marie Curie

"Forgiveness of others is essential to mental peace and radiant health. You must forgive everyone who has ever hurt you if you want perfect health and happiness."
—Dr. Joseph Murphy

Beth McGill

Beth is a certified hypnotherapist, energy healer practitioner, spiritual mentor, teacher, inspirational speaker and best-selling author. She is also a self-proclaimed soul surfer! Her deepest desire is to help you understand who you really are and your purpose for being here, and to help provide you with the clarity, confidence and courage to live your life as the powerful creator that she knows you to be.

A few years ago, she began her spiritual journey by setting her phone timer for five minutes, quieting her mind, and asking God, "Who Am I?" She admits that she didn't know what she was doing at the time, but now knows that she was feeling the calling of her soul. She knew she was here on this planet for more—more joy, more abundance, more freedom—but she didn't know how to get it. Since then, she's figured out that it's not her job to know the "how." She believes that when you truly understand how powerful you are, you will surrender and let go of having to be in control. Then, you will allow life to happen and receive everything you desire. The Universe has it all figured out. Now, she is on a mission to help you live a life you love, standing in fearless faith, nonresistance and unconditional love. She's also passionate about helping you heal so that you can achieve optimum physical and emotional well-being.

Email: **thriveflourishgrow@gmail.com**
Phone: 805-441-5983
Website: **www.thriveflourishgrow.com**
Facebook: **https://www.facebook.com/inspiredbethmcgill**
LinkedIn: **https://www.linkedin.com/in/bethmcgillccf/**
YouTube: **https://www.youtube.com/channel/UCnjVdY5dYysh8NESMW9c4Fw**
Instagram: **https://www.instagram.com/bethmcgillthriving/**

DISCOVER YOUR CREATIVE POTENTIAL
BY BRI CAPIRSI

You're living and breathing on Earth right now. Your soul entered and survived being in a physical body, so now what? Are you feeling emotionally intense, like you don't know what you're doing here on this weird planet? Good, this is all about you and your beliefs, about your own purpose for being here, and it has nothing to do with anybody else. For the rest of your life, you could look to another to tell you what you should do to feel more aligned, to feel more passionate, to feel "happier" while living here. Well, what I've learned through my journey is that the only person who really has that answer is you. The way to find it is to tap in and listen to your soul, your intuition and your own needs. The truth is, I didn't heal my body or my life until I stopped listening to everybody else. I have very strong beliefs that you can heal your life experience in the very same way, which is why I'm here to share this with you. Here are my thoughts on the joy and healing of finding the unique energetic makeup of yourself. I sure hope you find it supportive on your life path.

My Personal Story

For the first twenty-seven years of my life, I was sick with a mystery illness that doctors couldn't diagnose. My body would randomly convulse, but it was never classified a seizure. My legs would collapse to the ground, and at times I would need others to push me around in a wheelchair for hours until muscle tone eventually came back to my legs. After testing me over and over again and getting second opinions, medical professionals all pretty much came to the conclusion that I was doing it for attention. From the physical world, and from what they saw from their point of view, I was completely healthy, so they assumed I must have had a mental health problem.

In my personal case, what I really had was an energetic problem. When I started tapping into my intuition and my needs after deeply releasing on a soul level, I noticed that these neurological episodes happened whenever there were spirits from the other side trying to get my attention, or whenever I was absorbing too much energy from others in the room. I could hear spirits talking to me in my ears! I was having severe neurological problems because I didn't know how to channel my energy correctly through my body. I didn't know how to protect and manage my energy field. As soon as I found and learned how, through visual meditation and other energy management practices, my episodes and neurological problems completely disappeared. I was able to heal myself! Stand, walk and function normally, healthfully and powerfully.

1st Key Point: The Importance of the Emotional Self

When's the last time you were truly in touch with your emotions? This could be the key to knowing how unaligned you are in your life and with your work. If you're someone who uses alcohol and drugs, it's possible you haven't felt the unique inner spark that is you in a very long time. If you're someone that takes prescribed medication to make your intense feelings go away and you feel a bit numb, it's possible you're also someone who has no idea where your soul is leading you. If you're someone who overworks yourself to the point where you don't have time to look at your emotions and forget that you even have them, this is another sign that you could be out of alignment with your soul or intuition. I've been there, so I see you. It's difficult, I know! Putting away the emotions or numbing them makes handling the physical realities of Earth easier, which is why we tend to do it, but what I've found is we really can't continue doing that long-term because it causes sickness to build up within our bodies. If you are a highly sensitive creative empath like me, this is even more so the case.

Your energy body is linked to your emotions. We have emotions for a reason: they are our north compass leading us to places we want to go and away from places that are harmful to us or unaligned with who we are. If we cope and shut them down daily, they build up inside of us and cause even more chaos until we are at the point where they seem so big and daunting that we just don't know what to do about them anymore! I personally believe this is how we lose many to suicide and overdoses in the world. I have walked the tightrope of life and death myself. When we have intense feelings of self-destruction, it is not supposed to be a terribly awful thing to hold onto. It is often just a part of the process of spiritually awakening to the truest parts of yourself and your energy.

2nd Key Point: How Can We Manage Our Energy Body Naturally?

On my journey as a highly sensitive person, I've learned that you don't need to cope with any substances or partake in escapism practices to be able to manage your emotions or energy body naturally. I was able to tap into my energy body through deep release practices. I went to many facilitated grief rituals to cry out all the tears of my trauma. I went to a therapist who was certified in Eye Movement Desensitization Reprocessing therapy and unraveled chaotic belief systems I had created in my life that allowed a lot of my internal chaos to fall out of my body. I and others I know have also gone to emotional release therapy professionals, Reiki Masters and shamanic practitioners to obtain the same goal.

Through these deep release practices, I finally got to the point where I no longer felt the anxiety in my chest daily. I was actually able to notice what I was feeling from moment to moment. I was able to listen to my intuition! The magical moments and synchronicities started to happen to me daily after this, because I was noticing my inner connection to source and all that is. My feelings were communicating to me the opportunities I wanted to take and the lessons I needed to learn. I started having psychic experiences, I started healing my own body, and I started knowing exactly where my soul was aligned, and also where it wasn't. Now, I run a spiritual-based practice as an intuitive astrologer and physical medium. I'm a musician, an author, a podcaster, and a teacher of emotional processing and transmuting to highly sensitives. I creatively express to others my authentic experience of what it's like to be me on this planet. It perfectly aligns with my specific energy. I'm happy to report I've been able to set healthy boundaries and communicate to others with confidence what is and isn't right for me, and I've been able to show up in my life from a place of personal power and in a body that is no longer sick. I've also been able to support and empower others in doing the same.

3rd Key Point: Your Unique Energetic Design

I am now able to energetically read others around me with my gifts. What I have discovered is that we all have a very specific energetic design that is unlike anybody else's. We might have certain parts of our energy that are similar to others, but no one is ever exactly the same. This is what makes us feel individual and special, but it can also be what isolates us from others, when we have that nagging part that is pulling and tugging at us to wake up to share our own unique brilliance with the world.

In my opinion, everyone is here to discover their own creative potential, to tap into their intuition and their divine gifts. After finding and cultivating these gifts, we feel empowered to use them to support loved ones or the collective in some way. We find self-love and fulfillment by doing this. This is what happens when we get in touch with our soul, with our divine connection to all that is. It doesn't matter what your spiritual beliefs are, most align with the idea that you are here to serve and connect with others and to feel safe and bright as you live in your light.

4th Key Point: Self-Love, Balance, and Integration

Based on what I've experienced, I see life as a process of balance and integration. You are a superhuman if you are able to make it through life having complete control over everything you experience without chaos ensuing. Life is a process of rises and falls, and if you're tuned in to your energy, you're able to ride the waves much easier. You can work to balance the aspects of the physical, mental and emotional bodies as you move through life experience based on what you're actively experiencing. You can have a greater sense of what you need day to day, moment to moment, if you are tapped into your physical, mental and emotional bodies.

I believe in the neverending flow of the river of life. You have to go down the river if you want to be alive in this body. You have a set of energetic instructions, and it's a map. It tells you where the big boulders are going to be, where the twists and turns are going to take you, where the big waterfalls are and where the weather will be bad. Inevitably, you have to flow with it all if you want to stay on the river. You can choose to leave the river anytime, or you can choose to hop in that raft for the ride of your life. You have a lot of decisions to make on this planet while you're here. So tell me, how are you going to ride the waves? We are multidimensional beings. We are frequencies, songs of the universe. As we speak, we sing our own unique song. The energy centers in us light up, one by one, based on what we decide to choose, say and experience. We sing new songs every day, and these songs are creating aspects of our life. We are incarnated on this beautiful planet, with her own unique frequency, co-creating with her as well. Our light bodies inside these weird watery meat suits are far-reaching, way farther out than we can ever really see, and we are pulled every day by the lights and frequencies of each other and the lights and frequencies of the galaxy, much like that age-old notion that our bodies made of water are pulled and affected by each full moon. This is what I see through my eyes and what I hope is expanding your vision to fully embrace all that you are.

It might seem like a daunting and lengthy process to choose to dive deep into your emotions to release them and figure out the nature of who you truly are as an energy being. You'd likely have to make a lot of time and space for it in the way you live your life right now. You'd have to take action and be accountable to make a lot of changes about how you use your energy. My advice to you is to look at everything and everyone around you that you deeply care about. Question: is not showing up currently as your best and brilliant self serving them, or you? Think of the nature of your conflicts, the boundaries you don't know how to set because you don't know where to set them, and then think of the pain that causes. Think of the problems that continue to be thrown your way over and over again, and think about how you're not quite sure how to solve them. Imagine that you suddenly had the knowledge, because you deeply released what doesn't serve you and plugged back into what really matters to your soul. Imagine that you know who you are and what you're here to create and contribute, and who to create and contribute with. Then imagine the immense healing and profound magic you experience following this transformation when you feel a greater connection to all that is.

I am a living testament, having discovered the magic of my brilliance these past few years. I invite you to deeply release your emotions, to transform, to find self-love and balance regarding your physical, mental and emotional bodies, and then to go and live your unique brilliance alongside me, too. I am cheering you on! Share and shine as the wonderful and unique gift that you are!

INSPIRATIONAL QUOTES PROVIDED BY BRI CAPIRSI

"I spent a long time trying to find my center until I looked closely one night and found it had wheels and moved easily in the slightest breeze, so now I spend less time sitting and more time sailing."
—Brian Andreas

"Prayer is not asking. It is a longing of the soul. It is daily admission of one's weakness . . . And so, it is better in prayer to have a heart without words than words without a heart."
—Gandhi

"If you want to be truly understood, you need to say everything three times, in three different ways. Once for each ear . . . and once for the heart."
—Paula Underwood Spencer

"We are so unused to emotion that we mistake any depth of feeling for sadness, any sense of the unknown for fear, and any sense of peace for boredom."
—Mark Nepo

"The energies I've been running from are the very ones that hold the deepest truths, and the deepest love. Fear has been a door to the dreams I wish I could make real while I sit in the illusion of everything in this life that seems so fulfilling and fun."
—Bri Capirsi

"Don't ever let anyone else tell you what your identity is. Create it out of all of your unique talents, experiences and ways of thinking. Write your story. Tell everyone what you see and what you've learned. You're a special part of the puzzle, and without you, we wouldn't know."
—Bri Capirsi

Bri Capirsi

Bri Capirsi is a highly intuitive creative from the enchanted forests of the Pacific Northwest. Having obtained a bachelor's degree in education, she has previously been an educator in various teaching settings supporting the development and growth of children. Bri's mysterious health journey has led her to study Celtic shamanic practices, spiritual theory, mediumship, western intuitive astrology and other light magic for the past seven years. Her ability to process energy and integrate aspects of the mind, body and soul experience for soul-growth purposes has healed her own illnesses and insecurities, sparking a flame in her to assist other highly sensitives in healing their experiences, too. As a musician, a writer, a podcaster, an astrologer, and an energy healer through her online business practice, Bri uses aspects of intuition and creativity in her daily routines and teaches others how they too can naturally process and integrate their emotions as part of their routines for overall wellness. She currently resides with her family in the mountains near Salt Lake City, Utah.

Email Address: **bricapirsi@gmail.com**
Phone Number: 253-329-8339
Website:
https://**starseermysteries.com**
Facebook:
https://www.facebook.com/starseerm/
https://www.facebook.com/starseermyst/
Twitter:
https://twitter.com/StarseerM
YouTube:
https://www.youtube.com/@starseermysteries
Instagram:
https://www.instagram.com/starseer.mysteries/
TikTok:
https://www.tiktok.com/@starseermysteries
Spotify Podcast:
Applied Astrology & the Highly Sensitive Experience **https://open.spotify.com/show/1YPgAeJNhEr6BKfM7e4kix?si=9429793fa5aa4a55**

SECTION 3:

Share Your Brilliance

LEADERSHIP OF SELF:
HOW WE SHOW UP IS A CHOICE
BY DR. CHERYL LENTZ

Many people discuss leadership, referring to the leadership *of others*. Often forgotten is the importance of leading ourselves first. Forgotten is the knowledge that leadership is a choice to decide how we want to show up and how we want to be seen. This is a leadership story of the choice of how I choose to show up in my own life each and every day.

Leadership can be risky, which is why many decide they would rather follow than lead. The result of remaining a follower is lack of personal accountability, lack of ownership, and the ability to blame others if something doesn't go as expected or as wanted. We forget that leadership is a choice of whom we follow as well as how we might choose to lead others. The concept of others must first and foremost refer to ourselves, however. Why would others choose to follow us if we don't choose to follow ourselves?

Interesting question to consider, isn't it?

The question to think about is what happens when we don't show up as we want.

I didn't.

What happens when things don't go as we expected, planned, or hoped?

Things didn't.

The choice is ours alone. Often when we fail in leadership, we fail ourselves. I know this failure firsthand because I didn't choose to lead me, either. The question really is how much of a failure we want to remain.

How Did I Get Here?

Life really handed me lemons—a whole bunch of them. I was mad. I was frustrated. I was overwhelmed. I didn't know how I got here. I couldn't go back, and I wasn't going forward. I became ill. Very ill. *Mayo-Clinic-we-don't-know-why-you're-sick* kind of ill. So sick, I could barely stand for five minutes in front of the stove to cook dinner.

I didn't see this coming.

I remember thinking this must be how a computer works. With so many different commands being entered in contradiction by so many, in a state of confusion and frustration, the motherboard just stopped and shut itself down.

Poof!

One day, I couldn't get out of bed. My body simply stopped working. AND as if that wasn't bad enough, no one could tell me why.

I spent spring break at Mayo Clinic, leaving with no less than forty-eight holes in me from various tests. They prodded and stuck me, performing everything from muscle integrity tests to biopsies to find out why the body had just shut off.

Many theories. Little evidence. No answers.

I went home feeling very much like a garden hose. I could have twirled and watered my lawn.

I felt useless. I was in pain. My life was falling apart, and I had no idea why.

Rainbows Come After the Rain

The law of attraction offers that we will attract that which we are at the frequency of our vibration. I couldn't accept that I was doing this to myself on some level. What was going on inside that would attract such misery? Why did the body shut down? What was going on that no one could figure out? If the medical profession couldn't find the answers, someone had to know. I was determined to find that person who knew and give them a piece of my mind. Yep, I had had enough. I wanted to surrender with a white flag in hand. This had to stop, and now. I was on a quest. I was determined to find them.

The shocking discovery was that the person who knew the answers was me all along. I knew. My body knew. My body always knew.

The solution was actually in surrendering, ironically.

How could I miss something of such importance? I never thought to even ask the question. I never asked *me* what was wrong. I wouldn't have been tuned in to listen if I had. I never realized that the Universe had been sending me messages for quite some time and I wasn't paying attention.

To get my attention, the Universe literally had to bring me to my knees.

And to my knees I fell.

Dim My Light?

During my doctoral journey, I remember my faculty teaching that it is in asking the right questions that the right answers will come. I didn't ask the right questions. Heck, I didn't ask my body any questions at all. I was only asking *external* questions, looking for *external* answers from that infamous person from whom I was seeking validation. I should have been asking *me* and looking within.

Since I wasn't asking, one would think there were no answers to listen to, and you would be wrong. The Universe had been sending me answers for quite some time. I wasn't listening. I didn't know how to listen. I didn't know whom to listen to. I missed the signs.

The Universe put me in a wheelchair to get my attention.

Get my attention it did. The Universe now had my UNdivided attention. I was forced to listen.

Gratitude

I am grateful for that wheelchair wake-up call. I wonder where I would be today without that horrible moment. There is nothing worse than feeling helpless. The one thing you should be able to control is your own body. Mine refused. I was so embarrassed and afraid, I trusted no one, least of all me.

I had a choice: either to dim my light and succumb to being the victim, or to choose to walk out of the valley of darkness in faith. I dared to make the most difficult journey of all . . . the journey into the abyss, the journey to the depths of pain, darkness and an ugliness that I had yet to conquer. The journey didn't require a plane, train or automobile. This journey was the most daring of all . . . the path inward to self.

Life Happens For Us

I could have decided to stay in that wheelchair. That was always a choice. It was certainly the path of least resistance. I could have avoided all the pain. I could have stayed the victim and stayed where I was. No one would have faulted me for it, either, least of all me. I have been ill since the day I was born. I always knew I was different. I knew I wasn't like other kids. I just never knew why.

I remember traveling to a conference in San Diego and dancing in that wheelchair. Yep—on the dance floor in front of God and everyone in all of my brilliance. The chrome added extra sparkle. *chuckle* I decided that if I was going to be in that wheelchair, so be it. I would accept my life and make the best of it, and see the world while on wheels.

Walking Out of the Darkness

I fought for every step of my recovery. In the beginning, I didn't know any better. I thought I simply had to fight my way out and fight my way back. This was the long way. I was too stubborn to know there was a better way that didn't require fighting at all. I had to choose me. I had to choose love. I had to choose forgiveness, not just of others but of self.

I once had big dreams. I was a salutatorian in junior high. I was valedictorian in high school. I was going places. I was going to change the world. I would be somebody someday. Everyone said so.

And then very little of the life I planned happened. I let everyone down. Instead of getting better, life got worse—much worse—and stayed worse for many years.

In 2016, I finally lost everything—my husband and I divorced, my Siberian husky George died unexpectedly, and I had nowhere to go because I was being kicked out of my house as a result of the divorce.

It was as if I was checking boxes. I divorced my husband. Check. My dog died. Check. Kicked out of my house. Check, check, and check. Loss was complete. I moved to Indianapolis, where my big sister, from when I was in college, allowed me and my remaining Siberian Husky, Gracie, to move in with her. Several months later, Anna died. **Checkmate.**

What a year that was. It felt like it was the worst year ever. I was wrong here, too.

That year was part of the big reset and my journey back to me. Step by step, I found my way back. I moved in with my parents until I found a house. After twenty-five years of marriage, I was on my own, still recovering from my illness, still looking for answers, and trying to take care of me and my dog, Gracie. It was a scary time. I was a hot mess if truth be told. I kept this private journey into the valley of darkness my own personal secret. Few in my inner circle knew. I trusted no one. I was afraid to lose what little I was clinging to that kept me going.

On the outside, I appeared professional, maintaining my academic career as a college professor as well as my business. Inwardly, I withdrew. If I didn't love me, why would anyone else? I didn't feel worthy, and, quite candidly, I wondered why I was still here. I had been rejected by nearly all the men in my life, and I took it personally. I felt I was bruised and broken. The world said so, and I believed them.

God—the Universe—however you define—and I had long talks about where I was and why, and where I wanted to go and why and how to get there. I learned much in this time.

My body shut down because my dreams shut down. I didn't have dreams anymore. I was too afraid because everyone and everything I trusted simply disintegrated before my eyes. I didn't trust anyone . . . least of all, and most important of all, I didn't trust me. I was responsible for the decisions that led to this moment. How, then, could I be trusted going forward to make better decisions?

Leadership Comes Softly

For many, leadership comes in grand gestures. Think of big transformational events with marching bands and bolts of lightning. So many were doing amazing things in the world, and I was supposed to be one of them. It was always supposed to be me.

Instead, I failed. I FAILED BIG in EVERY area of my life. In some areas, I failed multiple times.

I felt like an impostor and a hypocrite as I had been teaching people how to recover from failure much of my professional career. Yet, I hadn't been listening completely because I was not yet the big success I planned. Where was the dream life? I was supposed to be in love. I was supposed to be successful. I was supposed to be healthy. I was supposed to be happy.

Professor, take thy own advice, right?

Sometimes leadership comes softly instead. What I failed to realize is that love is a choice. Success is a choice. Health is a choice. Happiness is a choice. This choice all starts with the self. I didn't love me; why then would, could, or should anyone else love me?

Reasonable question to ask.

In time, I learned the answer. The answer was that I was brilliant just the way I was. I had to stop dimming my light and step up and tell others to wear sunglasses instead. The answer was choice. The choice was to choose me, each and every day, each and every time. The choice was to love me. The choice was to be happy first, then happy things would come. Happy people would come. A happy life would come. Simple. Easy.

Dare to Show Up Differently

> *"Everything is energy and that's all there is to it.*
> *Match the frequency to the reality you want*
> *and you cannot help but get that reality. It can be no other way.*
> *This is not philosophy. This is physics."*
> —Albert Einstein

The laws of the Universe are infallible. They must happen. If we show up differently, often others will show up differently as well. It was risky. People might not choose me. And sometimes they didn't. I learned to show up differently, to be my authentic self, and to risk being just me. I decided to stop playing small.

When things happen, I ask for the lesson. I believe in me, even when others don't.

I would like to tell you that I fixed everything. Still working on it. I would like to tell you I'm married or at least in a committed relationship. I am not. I would like to tell you I'm setting the world on fire in the business world. I am not. Yet, I remain hopeful that someday I will find my path to both.

What I can tell you is that I am no longer in a wheelchair and haven't been for more than nine years. I kayak. I dance. I walk my dog. I can walk for more than five minutes. Success has come slowly for me. I still earn and choose respect of self and love of self each and every day.

Easy? Not always. Simple? Yes.

Lessons remain for us all. I will continue moving forward. Will you? I'm nothing special, I assure you, but I am worthy of knowing and worthy of love regardless of what the world or others may think. I am good enough.

You're pretty awesome, too. Choose you, okay?

Know that I'm here if you need help. I'm not perfect. I don't yet have the life I want or hoped to have, but I'm working on it. And that's a pretty okay place to be.

Believe in yourself. I do. Choose to love you. Choose you every day.

INSPIRATIONAL QUOTES PROVIDED BY DR. CHERYL LENTZ

"Plan your work; work your plan."
—Dr. Cheryl Lentz

"Choose the most effective tool for the most effective outcome."
—Dr. Cheryl Lentz

"Fail Faster, Succeed Sooner."
—Dr. Cheryl Lentz

"Don't dim your light. Invite others to wear sunglasses!"
—Dr. Cheryl Lentz

Dr. Cheryl Lentz

Dr. Cheryl Lentz, known as the Academic Entrepreneur, is a unique and dynamic speaker who intensely connects with her audience, having one foot in academia and one foot in the business and entrepreneurial space. Her goal is to offer the audience pearls of wisdom today they can use tomorrow in their personal and professional lives. It is not enough to know; the expectation is for participants to take action and do. Join Dr. Cheryl on her journey to connect these dots to provide inspiration, knowledge and counsel to move forward effectively.

Known globally for her writings on leadership and failure, as well as critical and refractive thinking she has been published more than fifty-eight times with twenty-six writing awards. As an accomplished university professor, speaker and consultant, she is an international best-selling author and a top quoted publishing professional on ABC, CBS, NBC and Fox. She took the stage as a speaker at TEDx Farmingdale on October 10, 2020.

>TEDx appearance: **https://www.youtube.com/watch?v=PbHlUPn7arQ**
>Social handles:
>**https://twitter.com/DrCherylLentz**
>**https://www.facebook.com/Dr.Cheryl.Lentz**
>**https://www.linkedin.com/in/drcheryllentz/**
>**https://www.youtube.com/drcheryllentz**
>**https://www.instagram.com/drcheryllentz/**
>Website: **http://DrCherylLentz.com**
>Email: **drcheryllentz@gmail.com**

SHARE YOUR GIFTS WITH THE WORLD: INTERVIEW LIKE A PRO
BY REBECCA HALL GRUYTER

"People will forget what you said, people will forget what you did, but people will never forget how you made them feel."
—attributed to Maya Angelou

The most impactful and personally rewarding strategies you can invest in to increase your visibility is simply by allowing people to see you, hear you, feel you and learn from you. I have seen hundreds of expert, heart-centered entrepreneurs grow their businesses through speaking. My favorite way to reach out and make an impact on a lot of people (and a great way to break into speaking on stage) is in the guest interview space.

From hosting, producing and leading multiple weekly online radio/TV shows a week over the past nine years, I have found that most people don't know how show up effectively to really share and shine as a guest expert.

There are so many podcast and virtual interview opportunities that are now available . . . it provides a powerful opportunity for experts to share their gifts and message. There are more shows and opportunities that experts can have easy access to than in years past. Yet, with all this opportunity, I find most experts don't have a plan of what to do before, during or after their appearance. They become really busy at times with interviews . . . but haven't really been able to harness them to grow their list, reach the people they want to reach and really, fully leverage each interview appearance. This means they are missing opportunities . . . working harder . . . and reaching fewer people. They aren't fully leveraging all the amazing content they are creating and the visibility opportunities that they could have . . . if only they had a plan. Your time, energy, gifts and talents are important. We want to help you be strategic in how you spend them so you can truly harness the visibility you are leaning into by choosing to share your message/information through interviews.

To support you in developing a plan to support you, here are my show-tested top seven tips to be your absolute best and leverage the opportunity of being a Guest Expert interviewed on a radio show, podcast, summit or other show format.

I'm going to share with you tips that will help you on a live interview show; however, you'll find these insights will be valuable whenever you speak in public. There is an art to showing up really well, like a pro. Learning these tips and putting them into practice will not only help you show up powerfully and like the pro you are . . . but also make you a great guest that hosts will want to ask back again and again.

Pro Tip #1: Prepare what you want to share with your viewers/listeners.

It's easy to feel nervous and, in the moment, forget even the most familiar information! Preparing ahead what you want to share will help you focus and not leave out anything important to you.

Write your ideas down into chunks that you can share in 90 seconds. Order them into bullet points that will help you remember the main points during the interview. You could also make a list of questions you would like to be asked (the host may ask you to submit some so you'll be ready). This is a good way to condense your ideas into questions and then answer them with your "sound bites."

Don't memorize! This is a live interview, a conversation—not a presentation. You want to be flexible so that you can respond to your host without feeling stuck in your script.

Just before a show (or any public appearance you make), take a moment to ground yourself and breathe. Then listen and feel into whether there's anything more to add to the list that you are called to share today. Trust the answer you receive. Remember that you are in service to the people who are watching/listening to you. And how you make them feel is more important than the exact words you say.

Pro Tip #2: When less is more . . .

The biggest mistake I see is a guest who talks too much! They get so excited about sharing that they get caught up and forget who's listening/watching. Time moves much faster than you think!

During your interview, make your responses in those sound bites of 90 seconds or less. Why is this?

- You want the energy to change throughout the show, so you can keep your audience engaged, informed and entertained. You don't want them to get lost or lose interest in a long, rambling answer.
- You make the greatest impact if you can describe your points succinctly. It's good practice whenever you talk about your work.
- Your host has a format and a schedule to follow, where there are ad breaks in the show that have to be honored. (Remember, this is the host's show. Allow them room to lead and to take breaks as needed to honor their show format.)

Pro Tip #3: Be respectful of the host's space.

You are on their show as their guest. Act as if you were a guest in their home.

You might not realize what it's like for them on their side of the desk. Often there are a lot of moving parts they are managing: preparing their intros, timing the segments, taking calls or comments in chat, dealing with tech or engineering, managing the conversation with an eye for the flow of the show, managing countdowns to commercials and bringing the show to a close successfully, to name just a few potential distractions.

How to be a mindful guest:

- Remember that even an experienced host may also be nervous. Be respectful of their space.
- Listen carefully to the question; don't interrupt or talk over the host.
- Allow them to run the conversation. Share your piece, then hand the ball back to them.
- If you think they are repeating a question, sometimes they just want you to go deeper. Just say, "Here's what I would like to add," and expand your answer.
- Don't use the phrase, "May I add one more thing?" and continue talking. Listen for their answer and be open to their saying no—remember, they are managing the time for the show.
- Extend grace to the host as they hold space for you, their listeners/viewers, and everyone and everything else that's involved in producing the event.

Pro Tip #4: Prepare yourself for success.

When you are invited to be interviewed, whether it's on a show, on stage, or any in-person format, do these things:

- Become familiar with the host—look at their website and social media presence.
- Listen to one or two shows prior to your interview date, so you get a feel for the flow.
- Prepare an introduction for the host, with the parts of your bio that fit the show. Remember that on-air time is precious, so keep it succinct!
- Ask your questions ahead of time. Not an hour prior to the show . . . or as the show is just starting . . . but a week in advance is great timing. Your questions might include: Am I able to make an offer? Share a link? If yes, what do you need me to provide you?
- Ask what information they want from you ahead of time. If they want questions, provide them. Honor their structure and flow.
- Always have a free gift available (make sure the host is okay with you sharing one) with a URL that is easy to read on air. When people sign

up for your free gift, it should add them to your list. This is a great way to expand your reach, serve the listening audience and grow your list.

Pro Tip #5: Be aware and intentional about how you are speaking.

Most of us speak very fast when we're talking among friends. When you speak in public, slow your pace down a little bit. Your audience needs time to absorb the important things you are saying, to feel into it and lean in for more. So speak clearly and slowly, and let what you say land.

If a glitch or distraction happens during the interview, it's okay to pause. Just take a breath, relax and move on. You'll be fine—because you trust you are the expert, you know the information and you are prepared.

Show up professionally and sit up attentively even if the show is not videotaped. This helps you keep your energy up and support your voice. Use the range of your voice to keep your audience engaged—this is something you can practice at home by just recording your voice on your phone, then listening for ways to sound strong and engaging.

Pro Tip #6: Build in promoting the show before and after the interview.

Many guests make the mistake of thinking the main event is the interview itself, and once it's complete the opportunity is over. In actuality, you have great visibility opportunities you can harness by promoting the show beforehand and after . . . and you can even share it strategically months later when the subject fits a monthly theme or ties into a speaking engagement or summit you are doing. You can keep using and repurposing the interview strategically.

I have found that approximately 90 to 95 percent of listeners actually like to listen on demand . . . so not necessarily when the interview is being produced live or pre-recorded, but when it is convenient for them to listen to it. If you neglect to share the replay out, you could be missing 90 to 95 percent of your potential listening audience.

- Promote the show beforehand in social media and to your list. Make sure to tag the interviewer so that they see you are promoting and sharing.

- Their followers will see you, too. This builds a great connection with the host.
- Add the replay of your show to your website. Media loves media. So the more other potential interviewers, people who are thinking of hiring/working with you, and events looking for guests can see that you have been on multiple programs and shows . . . and can see/experience a sample of you being interviewed. . . the more they can truly see and appreciate you and your expertise. Plus, this builds trust with other media platforms and show hosts, as they can now see you are able to hold the space positively and well. They tend to like to have guests on their shows who are experienced and know how to play well.
- Share the replay out in social media and with your followers. If you are too busy to share the replay out, then you are too busy to do the interview in the first place. The replay sharing is just as important as doing the interview itself. You want to actively promote and share the replay. Don't keep your fabulous interview that is showcasing you a secret. Share it out.
- Leveraging tips when sharing the replay:
  - Always tag the host so they can see you sharing out the show and partnering with them in getting the message out.
  - Add in a comment when you share out to create engagement . . . something like, "I loved the interview with XXX! My favorite part was . . . ." or "I shared a tip to help you XXXX." And then say, "I would love to know your thoughts about this." This gives them something to listen for and respond to.
  - And . . . even if people don't listen to the full show . . . they know simply by your sharing that you are a expert in your field who is in demand and a go-to person to interview and share about your area of expertise. ☺

Pro Tip #7: Have a plan for the interview—before, during and after.

This means know the type of shows you want to be on, schedule them in such a way that you are able to prepare ahead of time, be fully present during the interview, and be able to share the replay once the show has been recorded and the replay is available. Know why you are on the show, who you hope to serve . . . and how you will strategically share the replay of the show out after the show has officially aired.

- Be mindful of how many interviews you are scheduling a week/month/quarter . . . don't spread yourself too thin.
- Have a focus for each show. I recommend having a notecard or note page for each show that you can quickly refer to . . . showing what the show is about, your focus for the show (make sure it ties into what you are wanting to focus on that month), and whether you're offering a free gift (if so, note what it is). This way at a glance you can have all the key details of the show . . . including what you are focusing on talking about during your interview. Prepare this information when you schedule the interview . . . so you aren't left scrambling right before. You will come across professionally and in a expert or pro way, showing up clear, focused and prepared for the interview.
- Write out the three key bullet points you want to make sure you cover/discuss during the show . . . then review the notes a couple days prior to the show and the morning of. Then you will be fully and powerfully prepared.
- At the end of the show, take a few minutes to write down key thoughts from the interview that stood out for you. This way you will easily be able to refer back to that when you share the replay out . . . and if you want to share it down the road, you'll already know key points you can highlight to create powerful engagement.

Bonus Pro Tip:

Take a few minutes prior to the show to stop, pause, and breathe deeply. Remind yourself that you are the expert in this space and called to share this information. Trust that what will serve at the highest level will come forward in the conversation. You were made for such a time as this. As you breathe, release any anxiety/nerves. Remember, it is more about how you show up and hold the space than the exact words you say. Trust the interview process, and let your brilliance, heart and spirit SHINE!

INSPIRATIONAL QUOTES PROVIDED BY REBECCA HALL GRUYTER

"Be yourself; everyone else is already taken."
—Oscar Wilde

"Two roads diverged in a wood, and I-I took the one less traveled by, And that has made all the difference."
—Robert Frost

"The only place success comes before work is in the dictionary."
—Vince Lombardi

"Life is 10% what happens to me and 90% of how I react to it."
—Charles Swindoll

"You miss 100% of the shots you don't take."
—Wayne Gretzky

"When everything seems to be going against you, remember that the airplane takes off against the wind, not with it."
—Henry Ford

"Most people fail in life not because they aim to high and miss, but because they aim too low and hit."
—Lee Brown

"You become what you believe."
—Oprah Winfrey

"I'm a success today because I had a friend who believed in me and I didn't have the heart to let them down."
—Abraham Lincoln

"Promise me you will always remember: you're braver than you believe, and stronger than you seem, and smarter than you think."
—Christopher Robin to Winnie the Pooh, as written by A.A. Milne

"In the middle of difficulty likes opportunity."
—Albert Einstein

"All our dreams can come true, if we have the courage to pursue them."
—Walt Disney

"You were designed for accomplishment, engineered for success, and endowed with the seeds of greatness!"
—Zig Ziglar

"The question isn't who is going to let me; its who is going to stop me."
—Ayn Rand

"Start where you are. Use what you have. Do what you can."
—Arthur Ashe

"Act as if what you do makes a difference. It does."
—William James

"Problems are not stop signs, they are guidelines."
—Robert Schuller

"God's work done in God's way will never lack God's supplies."
—Hudson Taylor

QUOTES BY REBECCA HALL GRUYTER

"Life is not a Solo Journey."
—Rebecca Hall Gruyter

"Be willing to bloom where you are planted and SHINE!"
—Rebecca Hall Gruyter

"Choose to live on purpose and with purpose."
—Rebecca Hall Gruyter

"The greatest gift you can give the world is more of you. Choose to share the gift of you; SHINE!"
—Rebecca Hall Gruyter

"You must be willing to be seen on the same level you want to serve."
—Rebecca Hall Gruyter

Rebecca Hall Gruyter

Rebecca Hall Gruyter is a global influencer, a #1 international best-selling author, a compiler and publisher (helping over 900 authors become best sellers), a radio show host (reaching over 1 million listeners on 8 networks), and an empowerment leader. She has built multiple platforms to help experts reach more people. These platforms include radio, podcasts, books, magazines, the Speaker Talent Search, and live events, creating a powerful promotional reach of over 10 million!

Rebecca is the CEO of RHG Media Productions, the founder of Your Purpose Driven Practice, and the creator of the Speaker Talent Search. Rebecca has personally contributed to 40+ published books and multiple magazines, and she has been quoted in major media including Huffington Post, ABC, CBS, NBC, Fox, and Thrive Global. Today, she wants you to be seen, be heard, and SHINE!

http://www.YourPurposeDrivenPractice.com
http://www.RHGTVNetwork.com
http://www.SpeakerTalentSearch.com
Rebecca@YourPurposeDrivenPractice.com
http://www.facebook.com/rhallgruyter
http://www.facebook.com/pages/Rebecca-Hall-Gruyter/442052769207010
http://www.linkedin.com/pub/rebecca-hall-gruyter/9/266/280
http://www.twitter.com/Rebeccahgruyter
https://www.instagram.com/rhgtvnetwork/
http://www.EmpoweringWomenTransformingLives.com
http://www.rebeccahallgruyter.linktoexpert.com/

Quotes to Encourage and Inspire You

INSPIRATIONAL QUOTES PROVIDED BY WENDY HOOTON

"You never know how strong you are, until being strong is your only choice."
—Bob Marley

"Making a big life change is scary, but know what's even scarier? Regret."
—Zig Ziglar

"You weren't rejected. I hid your value from them because they were not assigned to your destiny.'"
—Unknown

"I've learned that people will forget what you said, people will forget what you did, but people will never forget how you made them feel."
—Maya Angelou

"Kindness is a gift everyone can afford to give."
—Unknown

At the end of each day Wendy Hooton asks herself: "What made me smile today? What are three things I'm grateful for? Did I live today, love today, matter today?"

INSPIRATIONAL QUOTES PROVIDED BY MISTI MAZURIK

"Life is not measured by the number of breaths we take, but by the moments that take our breath away."
—Maya Angelou

"There are three ways to ultimate success: The first way is to be kind. The second way is to be kind. The third way is to be kind."
—Mister Rogers

"Perfection is not attainable. But if we chase perfection we can catch excellence."
—Vince Lombardi

"The way I see it, if you want the rainbow, you gotta put up with the rain."
—Dolly Parton

"The two most important days in your life are the day you are born and the day you figure out why."
—Mark Twain

"Nothing is impossible. Even the word itself says, 'I'm possible!'"
—Audrey Hepburn

"Broken just means that there are more pieces to share."
—Misti Mazurik

INSPIRATIONAL QUOTES PROVIDED BY BEVERLY BRUNELLE

"I am unmoved by circumstances, therefore circumstances move."
—Florence Scovel Shinn

"I am awake to my good and my good is awake to me."
—Florence Scovel Shinn

"My good comes from expected and unexpected sources."
—Florence Scovel Shinn

"My good now flows to me in a steady, unbroken, ever-increasing stream of success, happiness and abundance."
—Florence Scovel Shinn

My source of inspiration is often self inquiry because the right question in the moment can open new possibilities.
If I were boldly honest with myself....

What am I assuming? How do I truly feel?
In an ideal world what would I prefer, want, need?
What questions will invite new possibilities?
What higher vibrational magic am I capable of?

QUOTES BY BEVERLY BRUNELLE

"Your thoughts and feelings have the power to deeply nurture you. Be aware and make choices that please and perhaps even surprise you."
—*Luminous Infusions,* Beverly Brunelle

"Call upon your future joy and success to guide you and act as a team."
—*Luminous Infusions,* Beverly Brunelle

"Let go to the experience of yourself unfolding. Make nothing wrong. Just open to it. Allow your self to be surprised."
—*Luminous Infusions,* Beverly Brunelle

INSPIRATIONAL QUOTES PROVIDED BY BETH MCGILL

"Let go of having to know HOW it's going to get done. The universe has it all figured out already. Don't be concerned about the outcome. Instead, allow life to happen for you and through you. Allow it all in —joy, abundance, success, prosperity, love and fun!"
—Beth McGill

"Manifesting and meditating cannot be separated. They are like the crest and the trough of the wave, separate and distinct from each other, but always together. You cannot become adept at manifesting the desires of your heart if you are unwilling to devote time to the practice of meditation."
—Wayne Dyer

"There is for each man, perfect self-expression. There is a place which he is to fill and no one else can fill, something which he is to do, which no one else can do; it is his destiny!"
—Florence Scovel Shinn

"People do not attract that which they want, but that which they are."
—James Allen

"Nothing in life is to be feared, it is only to be understood. Now is the time to understand more, so that we may fear less."
—Marie Curie

"Forgiveness of others is essential to mental peace and radiant health. You must forgive everyone who has ever hurt you if you want perfect health and happiness."
—Dr. Joseph Murphy

INSPIRATIONAL QUOTES PROVIDED BY BRI CAPIRSI

"I spent a long time trying to find my center until I looked closely one night and found it had wheels and moved easily in the slightest breeze, so now I spend less time sitting and more time sailing."
—Brian Andreas

"Prayer is not asking. It is a longing of the soul. It is daily admission of one's weakness . . . And so, it is better in prayer to have a heart without words than words without a heart."
—Gandhi

"If you want to be truly understood, you need to say everything three times, in three different ways. Once for each ear . . . and once for the heart."
—Paula Underwood Spencer

"We are so unused to emotion that we mistake any depth of feeling for sadness, any sense of the unknown for fear, and any sense of peace for boredom."
—Mark Nepo

"The energies I've been running from are the very ones that hold the deepest truths, and the deepest love. Fear has been a door to the dreams I wish I could make real while I sit in the illusion of everything in this life that seems so fulfilling and fun."
—Bri Capirsi

"Don't ever let anyone else tell you what your identity is. Create it out of all of your unique talents, experiences and ways of thinking. Write your story. Tell everyone what you see and what you've learned. You're a special part of the puzzle, and without you, we wouldn't know."
—Bri Capirsi

INSPIRATIONAL QUOTES PROVIDED BY DR. CHERYL LENTZ

"Plan your work; work your plan."
—Dr. Cheryl Lentz

"Choose the most effective tool for the most effective outcome."
—Dr. Cheryl Lentz

"Fail Faster, Succeed Sooner."
—Dr. Cheryl Lentz

"Don't dim your light. Invite others to wear sunglasses!"
—Dr. Cheryl Lentz

INSPIRATIONAL QUOTES PROVIDED BY REBECCA HALL GRUYTER

"Be yourself; everyone else is already taken."
—Oscar Wilde

"Two roads diverged in a wood, and I-I took the one less traveled by, And that has made all the difference."
—Robert Frost

"The only place success comes before work is in the dictionary."
—Vince Lombardi

"Life is 10% what happens to me and 90% of how I react to it."
—Charles Swindoll

"You miss 100% of the shots you don't take."
—Wayne Gretzky

"When everything seems to be going against you, remember that the airplane takes off against the wind, not with it."
—Henry Ford

"Most people fail in life not because they aim to high and miss, but because they aim too low and hit."
—Lee Brown

"You become what you believe."
—Oprah Winfrey

"I'm a success today because I had a friend who believed in me and I didn't have the heart to let them down."
—Abraham Lincoln

"Promise me you will always remember: you're braver than you believe, and stronger than you seem, and smarter than you think."
—Christopher Robin to Winnie the Pooh, as written by A.A. Milne

"In the middle of difficulty lies opportunity."
—Albert Einstein

"All our dreams can come true, if we have the courage to pursue them."
—Walt Disney

"You were designed for accomplishment, engineered for success, and endowed with the seeds of greatness!"
—Zig Ziglar

"The question isn't who is going to let me; its who is going to stop me."
—Ayn Rand

"Start where you are. Use what you have. Do what you can."
—Arthur Ashe

"Act as if what you do makes a difference. It does."
—William James

"Problems are not stop signs, they are guidelines."
—Robert Schuller

"God's work done in God's way will never lack God's supplies."
—Hudson Taylor

QUOTES BY REBECCA HALL GRUYTER

"Life is not a Solo Journey."
—Rebecca Hall Gruyter

"Be willing to bloom where you are planted and SHINE!"
—Rebecca Hall Gruyter

"Choose to live on purpose and with purpose."
—Rebecca Hall Gruyter

"The greatest gift you can give the world is more of you. Choose to share the gift of you; SHINE!"
—Rebecca Hall Gruyter

"You must be willing to be seen on the same level you want to serve."
—Rebecca Hall Gruyter

What Quotes Inspire You to Share Your Brilliance?

STEP INTO YOUR BRILLIANT PURPOSE

WHAT QUOTES INSPIRE YOU TO SHARE YOUR BRILLIANCE?

STEP INTO YOUR BRILLIANT PURPOSE

WHAT QUOTES INSPIRE YOU TO SHARE YOUR BRILLIANCE?

CLOSING THOUGHTS

We hope you have been touched by these powerful chapters that have encouraged, equipped, and empowered you to *Share Your Brilliance*! We can't wait to see you, hear from you, and celebrate you as you share your gift of you with the world! May you always choose to **live on purpose and with great purpose.**

Anthologies Compiled by Rebecca Hall Gruyter:

<u>SHINE Series</u> (compiled and led by Rebecca Hall Gruyter)
    Come Out of Hiding and SHINE! (Book 1)
    Bloom Where You Are Planted and SHINE! (Book 2)
    Step Forward and SHINE! (Book 3)

<u>Step Into Series</u> (compiled and led by Rebecca Hall Gruyter)
    Step Into Your Brilliance! (Book 1)
    Step Into Your Brilliant Purpose! (Book 2)
    Share Your Brilliance! (Book 3)

<u>Experts and Influencers Series</u> (compiled and led by Rebecca Hall Gruyter)
    Experts and Influencers Series: Leadership (Book 1)
    Experts and Influencers Series: Women's Empowerment (Book 2)
    Experts and Influencers Series: Step Forward With Purpose (Book 3)

The Grandmother Legacies (anthology compiled by Rebecca Hall Gruyter)

The Animal Legacies (anthology compiled by Rebecca Hall Gruyter)

Bloom & SHINE! (365 daily inspiration anthology compiled by Rebecca Hall Gruyter)

Empowering YOU, Transforming Lives (365 daily inspiration anthology compiled by Rebecca Hall Gruyter)

Journals by Rebecca Hall Gruyter:

The Animal Legacies Journal
The Experts and Influencers Leadership Journal
The Experts and Influencers Women's Empowerment Journal
The Experts and Influencers Move Forward With Purpose Journal
Women's Empowerment Journal
Step Into Your Brilliance Journal
Step Into Your Brilliant Purpose Journal
Share Your Brilliance Journal

Books Featuring a Chapter by Rebecca Hall Gruyter:

The 40/40 Rules, anthology compiled by Holly Porter
Becoming Outrageously Successful, anthology compiled by Dr. Anita Jackson
Bright Spots, anthology compiled by Davis Creative
Catch Your Star, anthology published by THRIVE Publishing
Discover Your Destiny, anthology compiled by Denise Joy Thompson
Engaging Experts, anthology compiled by Davis Creative
I Am Beautiful, anthology compiled by Teresa Hawley-Howard
Movers & Shakers 2020, anthology compiled by Teresa Hawley-Howard
The Power of Our Voices, Sharing Our Story, anthology compiled by Teresa Hawley-Howard
Real Estate Investing for Women, anthology compiled by Moneeka Sawyer
Succeeding Against All Odds, anthology compiled by Sandra Yancey
Success Secrets for Today's Feminine Entrepreneurs, anthology compiled by Dr. Anita Jackson
The Unstoppable Woman of Purpose, anthology and workbook, compiled by Nella Chikwe
Women on a Mission, anthology compiled by Teresa Hawley-Howard
Women of Courage, Women of Destiny, anthology compiled by Dr. Anita Jackson
Women Warriors Who Make It Rock, anthology compiled by Nichole Peters
You Are Whole, Perfect, and Complete—Just as You Are, compiled by Carol Plummer and Susan Driscoll

Dear Powerful Reader,

Thank you for reading our anthology. We hope it has encouraged and empowered you and uplifted you in the area of leadership. Listed below, please find out a little bit more about us.

RHG Media Productions and Your Purpose Driven Practice™

I wanted to share a little bit more about our organizations, Your Purpose Driven Practice™, RHG TV Network™, RHG Publishing™, and RHG Media Productions™. We are passionate about helping others live on purpose and with purpose in their lives and business. I hope this book has supported and inspired you to choose to live on purpose and with great purpose in your leadership!

If you want to reach more people and be part of inspiring and supporting others with your message, your gifts, and the work that you bring to the world, then I want to share some opportunities for you to consider.

Each year we compile and produce anthology book projects, support authors in publishing their own powerful books as bestsellers, produce and publish an international magazine, facilitate women's empowerment conferences, get quoted in major media, launch radio and podcast shows, and help experts and speakers step into a place of powerful influence to make a global difference. We provide programs and strategies to help you reach more people and facilitate the Speaker Talent Search (which helps speakers, experts, and influencers connect with more speaking opportunities). We would love to support you in reaching more people. Please take a moment to learn a little bit more about us at the sites listed below, and then reach out to us for a conversation. **We would love to help you be seen, be heard, and SHINE!**

You can learn more about each of these things on our main website: **www.YourPurposeDrivenPractice.com**

Enjoy our powerful **TV and podcast shows:** www.RHGTVNetwork.com

Learn more about the **Speaker Talent Search™:** www.SpeakerTalentSearch.com

Learn more about our **writing opportunities**: **http://yourpurposedriven practice.com/writing-opportunities/**

If you would like to connect with me personally to explore some of our opportunities in upcoming book projects, podcast/radio shows, and/or TV, then here is the link to schedule a time to speak with me directly: **www.MeetWithRebecca.com**, or you can email me at: **Rebecca@YourPuposeDrivenPractice.com**.

May you always choose to be seen, be heard, and SHINE!

Warmly,

Rebecca Hall Gruyter

www.ingramcontent.com/pod-product-compliance
Lightning Source LLC
Chambersburg PA
CBHW071020080526
44587CB00015B/2431